The House of Lords from the river.

THE

HISTORY

OF THE

Gun-Powder Plot:

WITH SEVERAL

HISTORICAL CIRCUMSTANCES
PRIOR TO THAT EVENT,

CONNECTING THE

PLOTS OF THE ROMAN CATHOLICS

TO

Re-Establish POPERY in This KINGDOM

Digested and Arranged from Authentic Materials,
by JAMES CAULFIELD

London
Spradabach Publishing
2024

Spradabach Publishing
BM Box Spradabach
London WC1N 3XX

The History of the Gun-Powder Plot:
with Several Historical Circumstances Prior to that Event,
Connecting the Plots of the Roman Catholics
to Re-Establish Popery in this Kingdom

First published in 1804
First Spradabach edition published 2024
© Spradabach Publishing 2024

Interior design by Alex Kurtagic

ISBN 978-1-909606-53-1

British Library Cataloguing-in-Publication Data:
A catalogue record for this book is available from the British Library.

Table of Contents

TABLE OF CONTENTS

ℭable of Illustrations

Note on This Edition

he text in this volume is based on the 1804 edition published in London by Vernor and Hood. The spelling, punctuation, capitalisation, and italics have been left as in the original, with some exceptions: inconsistent capitalisation of religious denominations, place names, etc. has been homogenised; the titles of works referred to in the text have been taken out of quotation marks and put in italics; also put in italics have been passages in Latin; and extensive quotes have also been taken out of quotation marks and set as block quotes.

A full index has been generated. In the latter, geographical names have been rendered as per their modern spelling (*e.g.*, Douai, rather than Douay, as in the text).

Advertisement

otwithstanding the many detached pieces extant, concerning the Gun-powder Treason, there is no one that regularly details the circumstances attendant on that affair; and, to this day, the whole is treated by some as a fable, for want of proper evidence to establish the facts, the Catholics having suppressed, as far as possible, every enquiry on this head. The following History is collected from almost every piece that has appeared on the subject; and particular care has been taken to introduce into the Biographical parts the material transactions relative to each person, in their proper places; and, in order more fully to explain the foundation of this plot, the subject is treated from its original source, namely, the Reformation, as begun by Henry the Eighth, with the proceedings of the Catholics under his successors, to the accession of James the First. The illustrations by Prints which accompany this Work, maybe: depended on in point of authenticity, as the publication of the originals from which they are copied, are coeval with the times they represent.

Henry the Eighth

enry the Eighth, the most turbulent and self-willed tyrant that ever lived, having to accommodate his passion for Anne Bullen (and not from a principle of religion,[1] as he pretended), thrown off the yoke

---

[1] That he lived and died a Papist, is evident, as it is well known that his last queen, Catharine Parr, who was a strict Protestant, by too eagerly opposing him in principles of religion, had nearly been sent to the Tower, which she only prevented by luckily finding some papers communicated to the king by Gardiner, bishop of Winchester, a most rigid, time serving priest, who actually came into a garden where they were discoursing on the subject of religion, which she had artfully introduced,

of Popery, proceeded to the dissolution of the religious houses in England, which giving offence to many Catholics of distinction, who were above dissimulation, they utterly refused to take the new oaths that were generally prescribed to persons in any kind of office, of acknowledging him supreme head of the Church; to those that refused, Henry was not content with discharging them from their employments, but made it high treason in the denial, and proceeded so far as to take off the heads of Sir Thomas More, and Fisher, bishop of Rochester, men of the first rank and ability, who were considered by the generality of the people as martyrs to the wanton caprice of a despotic tyrant. The deaths of these great men encreased the detestation of the Catholics against the king, and had he not done something, by bestowing the revenues of the dissolved religious houses on the creatures he had newly taken about him, to secure them in his interest, it is probable that the Catholics would have attempted something with success against

---

and entirely regained Henry's favour, by assuring him, that if ever she had contradicted him on that subject, it was only for the pleasure she took in hearing his powerful and satisfactory answers to her weak arguments: to this flattery she was at least indebted for her liberty, if not for her head, as, when Gardiner came forward with the warrant, signed by the king, for her imprisonment, Henry peevishly bade him begone, and, on the queen's soliciting him not to be angry with the "good bishop," he replied, that he deserved no favour at her hands, for the "good he intended her." The king's death, which happened soon after, entirely freed her from any fear on the score of religion.

his person. Priests, who were convicted in denying his supremacy, were punished with imprisonment; and, in one instance his resentment went so
far, as to cause a large estate to be taken from a
gentleman, for assisting a priest who was confined
in the gaol at Buckingham, with eight pence and
two shirts.

Edward the Sixth

uring the short reign of Edward the Sixth, the Catholics seem to have been very inactive, although under his government, the Protestant faith was more firmly established than in that of his predecessor. As the people, having been long used to the tyranny of monkish confessors, and monastic landlords, were not a little pleased to find their new masters convert useless monasteries, which were harbours for idle priests, into pleasant country seats, that enlivened and relieved the poor, instead of harrassing and oppressing them. But these golden days were of but short duration, as the death of the most accomplished and best of kings was followed by the accession of his eldest Sister, a woman educated, to abhor any innovation in the religion she professed.

Mary the First

he first use Mary made of her power was to displace all Protestant preachers, and supply their places with zealous Papists. She next commissioned Bonner, bishop of London, with other Catholic priests, to examine such persons as were suspected of heresy, in denying the tenets of the Catholic church; and the punishment inflicted on those convicted of this pretended crime was burning alive. Many of the highest character in the Church suffered by the flames, particularly Cranmer, archbishop of Canterbury; Ridley, bishop of London; Latimer, bishop of Worcester; Farrar, bishop of St. David's; Hooper, bishop of Gloucester, and many of inferior dignity in the church, besides an immense quantity of private persons: the whole of which, in this reign, that suffered death for religion, is computed at 260 persons.[1] The ex treme rigour that was adopted to establish pacy, served entirely to abolish it. As the people seemed more terrified into the practice, than to follow it by inclination: and the death of Mary gave them an opportunity of following the doctrine that pleased them best.

---

1   Asthe catalogue of Martyrs that suffered in this reign may not be unacceptable, I have transcribed it from ascarce sheet, printed anno 1590.

Elizabeth

lizabeth having been strictly educated in the Protestant faith, no sooner ascended the throne than she publicly declared her religious opinions, and promoted Matthew Parker to the See of Canterbury, who, as metropolitan of England, displaced Catholic preachers, and substituted those of the reformed religion in their places; then it was the papal fury broke into a flame; and Pope Pius the Fifth issued a bull, excommunicating the Queen, and all that adhered to her, which bull was meant to inflame the minds of the people against her, and encourage the re-establishment of Popery in her dominion; for which purpose a number of English Catholics were assembled at Douay, to take holy orders as priests, and from thence to return to their native places, and disseminate their dangerous principles. The circumstance of these missionaries poisoning the minds of the people in their religion and allegiance, caused an act to be passed, constituting it death for any seminary priest to be found in this kingdom. The following persons were taken, and, being convincted, suffered death accordingly:[1]

---

1   The Catalogue of Popish priests is taken from an old sheet without date.

1570		
Iohn Felton	August 8	in Paules Church yard
1571		
Iohn Story	June 1	at Tyburne
1573		
Thomas Woodhouse	June 19	at Tyburne
1577		
Cuthbert Mayne	Nouem. 29	at Launston
Iohn Nelson	Feb. 3	at Tyburne
1578		
Thomas Sherwood	Feb. 7	
1579, 1580		

Anno 1577, in the month of Ianuary, was published a Proclamation against Seminary Priests and Iesuits, and for calling home the Queenes subjects from forraigne Seminaries, where they remained vnder colour of studies.		
1581		
Euerard Hanse	July 31	at Tyburne
Edmund Campion		
Alexander Bryant	Decem. 1	at Tyburne
Ralphe Sherwyn		
1582		
Iohn Paine	April 2	
Thomas Ford		
Iohn Shert	May 28	at Tyburne
Thomas Cottam		
William Filby		
Luke Kirby	May 30	at Tyburne
Lawrence Iohnson		
William Lacy	August 22	at Yorke
Richard Kirkman		
Iames Thompson	in Nouem.	at Yorke
1583		
Richard Thirkhill	May 29	at Yorke
Iohn Slade	Octob. 30	at Winchester
William Hart		at Yorke
Iames Laburne		at Lancaster
William Carter	Jan. 11	at Tyburne
George Haddocke, Io: Mundine, Iames Fen, Thomas Emerford, & Iohn Nutter	Feb. 12	at Tyburne

1584		
Iames Bele	April 20	at Lancaster
Iohn Finch		
Richard White	Octo. 18	at Wrixam
This yeare also were 21 Iesuits and Seminary Priests banished the Realme, Ian 21.		
1585		
Thomas Aufield	July 16	at Tyburne
Thomas Webley		
Hugh Taylor		at Yorke
Marmaduke Bowes		
Margaret Clitherow	in March	at Yorke
N. Hamelton		at Yorke
Rob. Bicardine		
Edward Transam	Janu. 21	at Tyburne
Nich: Woodfine		
This yeare also were 32 Priests & Iesuits banished the Realme, Sep. 19.		
1586		
Richard Sergeant	April 20	at Tyburne
William Tompson		
Iohn Adams		
Iohn Low	Octo. 8	at Tyburne
Rob: Debdale		
Rob: Anderton		at Tyburne
William Marsden		
Francis Ingleby		at Yorke
Stephen Rowsam		at Gloucester
Iohn Finglow		

1587		
Thomas Pilchard	in March	at Dorcester
Iohn Sands		at Gloucester
Iohn Hamly		at Chard
Alexander Crowe		at Yorke
Robert Sutton		at Stafford
Edmund Sykes		
Gabriell Thimbleby		
George Dowglas		

William Deane	August 28	at Myle-end-greene
Henry Webley		
William Gunter	eodem die.	at the Theat:
Robert Morton		at Licolnshs-Inne Fields
Hugh More	eodem die.	
Tho: Acton, alias Holford	eodem die.	at Clarkenwell
Richard Clarkson		
Thomas Felton	eodem die.	at Hownslow
Rich: Leigh, Edward Shelley, Hugh Morgan, Rich: Flower, Robert Martyn, Iohn Rocke, & Margaret Wade	August 30.	at Tyburne
Edward Iames	Octob. 1	at Chichester
Ralph Crochet		
Robert Wilcockes		
Edward Campio	eodem die.	at Canterbury
Christo: Buxton		
Rob. Widmerpoole		
William Wigges	eodem die.	at Kingston
Iohn Robinson	eodem die.	at Ipswich
Iohn Weldon	October 5	at Mile-end-gr.
William Hartley		
Rich: Williams	eodem die.	at Halliwell
Robert Sutton	eodem die.	at Clarkenwell
William Spencer		
Edward Burdon		
Iohn Hewyt		
Rob: Ludham		
Richard Simpson		at Darby
Nicholas Garlicke		
William Lampley		at Gloucester

14

1589		
George Nichols, Rich: Yaxley, Tho: Belson, Hu: vp Richard	July 5	at Oxford
Iohn Annas		
Robert Dalby	March 4	in Fleet-street
Christopher Bales	eodem die.	in Gr:In:lane
Alexander Blake	eodem die.	in Smithfield
Nicholas Horne		
1590		
Myles Gerrad		
Francis Dickinson	Aprill 30	at Rochester
Anthony Myddleton	May 6	at Clarkenwell
Edward Iones	May 6	in Fleet street

15

1591	Decem. 10	in Grays Inn Fields
Edmund Gennings		
Swithin Welles		
Eustach White		
Pollydor Plasden	Decem. 10	
Bryan Lacy		at Tyburne
John Mason		
Sidney Hodgson	Iuly 2	
Momfort Scot		in Fleet street
William Dickenson	Iuly 7	
Ralph Milner		in Winchester
GeorgeBisley }		
Edmund Ducke		
Rich: Holiday		at Durham
Ioh: Hagge		
Rich: Hill ;		
William Pykes	Ianu. 22	at Dorchester
William Pattison	Feb. 21	at Tyburne
Tho. Portmore		in Paules Church yard
This yeare also in the moneth of Octob: was published a Proclamation against Priests and Iesuits.		
1592		
Roger Ashton	June 23	at Tyburne
1593		
Iames Burdon	March 25	at Winchester
Anthony Page	March 30	at Yorke
Ioseph Lampton	Iune 23	at Newcastle
William Dauis	in Septem.	at Beumaris
Edward Waterson		
William Harrington	Feb. 18	at Tyburne

1594		
John Cornelius Mo-hum'	Iuly 4	at Dorchester
Tho: Bosgraue		
Patricke Samon		
John Carey		
Iohn Ingram		at Newcastle
Thomas Boast		
Iames Oldbaston	March 3	at Tyburne
Robert Southwell		
1595		
Henry Walpole		
'Alexander Rawlins	Aprill 17	at Yorke
George Errington		
William Knight		at Yorke
William Gibson		
Henry Abbots		
William Freeman		
1596		
N. Auleby		
N. Thorpe		
1597		
John Buckley, alias Iones	Iuly 12	at S. Th. Wa:
1598		
Thomas Snow		
Christoph: Robinson		
Rich: Horner		at Yorke
N. Grimston		
N: Britton		
1599		
Math: Hayes		at Yorke

1600		
Christopher Wharton, with a namelesse Woman	May 18 July 21	at Yorke at S: Th: Wa:
Iohn Rigby Robert Nutter	in June	at Lancaster
Edward Thwinge Thomas Sprot	in July	at Lincolne
Thomas Hunt Thomas Palaser	eodem mense.	at Durham
John Norton N: Talbot	Febr. 21	at Tyburne
Iohn Pibush RogerFilcocke Marke Barkworth Anne Lyne	Feb. 27	at Tyburne
1601		
Robert Middleton Thurstan Hunt		at Lancaster
1602		
Francis Page Thomas Tichborne Robert Watkinson Iames Ducket	Aprill 29	at Tyburne
N: Harrison N: Bates	in Aprill	at Yorke
William Richardson	Feb. 27	at Tyburne

Edmund Campion

dmund Campion was born in London, where he had his first education in Christ Hospital. From whence he was sent to St. John's College in Oxford, and obtained considerable approbation, as an orator and disputant; in both which capacities he entertained Queen Elizabeth at a public act, when she visited that university. He made two excellent funeral orations, the first in English, on the Lady Dudley, wife of the Earl of Leicester; the second in Latin, on Sir Thomas White, the founder. He soon after changed his religion, and retired to Douay, where he took his bachelor of divinity's degrees. In 1573 he travelled to Rome, where he became a Jesuit, and was soon after sent by his superiors, as a missionary, into Germany, where he composed his Latin tragedy, called *Nectar and Ambrosia*, which was acted with great applause, in the presence of the Emperor. The last scene of his life was in England, where he was regarded as a dangerous adversary of the established church. In his way to London, the council appointed a paper to be set upon his hat, with great capital letters "CAMPION THE SEDITIOUS JESUIT;" and gave orders he should be brought through all the market-towns that lay in the way, to gratify the people with the sight of a man who had made so much noise: after much cruel torture on the rack, he was executed at Tyburn, December the first, 1581. His writings shew him to have been a man of various and polite learning. His *Decem Rationes*, written against the Protestant religion, have been solidly answered by several of our best divines. The original manuscript of his *History of Ireland* is in the British Museum.

Robert Parsons

obert Parsons (or Persons, in both which ways he wrote his name) was the son of a black-smith, at Nether-stoway, near Bridgwater in Somersetshire, where he was born in 1546; and, appearing to be a boy of extraordinary parts, was taught Latin by the Vicar of the parish, who conceiving a great affection for him, contributed to his support at Oxford, where he was admitted of Baliol College in 1563, and became remarkable as an acute disputant in Scholastic exercise, then muchin vogue: he continued at

Robert Parsons,
Prefect of the English Mission,
1579

Oxford, until the year 1574, when he was obliged to resign his situation of Dean in the College, under the charge of incontinency, and embezzling the College money.

He had till this time openly professed himself a Protestant, and was the first who introduced books of that religion into the College Library; but soon after his disgrace at Oxford, he went to London, and from thence through Antwerp to Louvain; where, meeting with father William Good, his countryman, he spent a week in the spiritual exer cises at the College of that order, and began to entertain an affection for it: but being desirous to study physic, he proceeded to Padua for that purpose, where he had not been long, before his restless disposition led him to visit Rome. This visit fixed him heartily a Jesuit, for, here meeting with some Englishmen of the order, he became so impatient to be among them, that he went back to Padua, settled his affairs there, and returning to Rome, May 1575 was chosen a member of the Society of Jesus, and admitted into the English College.

He was indeed framed by nature, as well as inclination, for this society, being fierce, turbulent, and bold; and he soon made a distinguished figure in it, for by his credit with the Pope, in 1579 he obtained a grant to convert an hospital Rome founded in Queen Mary's time, into a College or Seminary for the English, by the name of "Collegium de urbe," dedicated to the Holy Trinity and

St. Thomas [à Becket], where the Students were obliged to take the following oath:

"I, N. N. considering with how great benefits God hath blessed me, &c. do promise by God's assistance, to enter into holy orders as soon as I shall be fit, and to return to England to convert my countrymen there, whenever it shall please the Superior of this house to command me."

He had no sooner seen this College settled, and his friend father Allen chosen by his recommendation, rector of it, than he was appointed to go in quality of superior in a mission to England, in order to promote the Romish religion in that kingdom. Edmund Campion was joined with him, and other assistants, in this arduous province; and they managed matters so artfully that, notwithstanding the time of their departure from Rome, and the whole rout of their journey, and even their pictures had been sent to England before them, yet they found means by disguise to escape the strictest search that was made, and arrived safe in London.

Parsons travelled about the country to gentlemens' houses, disguised either in the habit of a soldier, a gentleman, a minister, or an apparitor; and by the help of his associates, he entirely broke the custom which had till then prevailed among the Papists of frequenting the Protestant churches, and joining in the service: and, if we may credit his assertion, every thing was ready for a general insurrection before Christmas. But all his desperate designs were defeated by the vigilance of Lord

Burleigh; and Campion being discovered, seized and imprisoned, Parsons, who was then in Kent, immediately crossed the water, and went to Rouen in Normandy, and in 1583 returned to Rome.

In 1588 we find him engaged in Spain concerning the invasion of England, and on the defeat of the Spanish armada, he left no means in his power untried, to invite that monarch to a second invasion; and when nothing effectual could be obtained that way, he endeavoured to raise a rebellion in England, and tampered with the Earl of Derby to appear at the head of it, who was afterwards poisoned, by his procurement, for the refusal. The death of his friend, Cardinal Allen, in 1594, occupied the whole of his attention towards his own promotion to the vacant purple; but being disappointed in his expectation he retired to Naples, and did not return to Rome, till after the death of Clement VIII. in 1606.

Onthe 10th of April, 1610, he was seized with a fever, of which he died on the 18th. Paul the 5th, as soon as he heard of his illness, indulged him in all the ceremonies usually granted to cardinals at the point of death. His body was embalmed and interred, pursuant to, his own request, in the Chapel of his College at Rome, close to that of cardinal Allen. A monument was soon after erected to his memory, with an inscription; a copy of which may be seen in Ribadineira's *Bibl. Soc. Jes.* under the letter, P.

Alexander Briant

lexander Briant was born in Somersetshire, studied at Oxford, and afterward at Douay; from whence he was sent into England in character of a missionary, in the reign of Elizabeth, anno 1581. He was imprisoned, and as Dod tells us, was cruelly treated while he was in the Tower, by thrusting needles under the nails of his fingers, to force him to a discovery of what was acting abroad against the Queen and government.[1]

---

[1] It was at this time strongly reported, that a plot was hatch-

He was a young man of singular beauty, and behaved at the place of execution with decent intrepidity. Executed Dec. 1, 1581.

---

ing in the English Colleges at Rheims and Rome, with no less a view than the total subversion of the national religion and government. The fears and jealousies of the people were more alive than usual at this juncture, as the Duke of Anjou was in the height of his courtship with the Queen.

Thomas Cottam

homas Cottam was born in Lancashire, studied some time at Brazen-Nose College, Oxford, and afterwards at Rheims, where he was ordained priest.

In 1580 he was sent on a mission into England, but was apprehended soon after his landing. Dr. Ely, a professor of the civil and canon law at Douay, happened to be at Dover when he was taken, and with great address contrived and effected his escape; but as this benevolent act was like to be attended with the ruin of him and his family, Cottam very generously surrendered himself to save his benefactor.

He was several times put to the torture in pris-
on, but could not be prevailed on to make any confession, or renounce his religion.

He and Briant are said to have been admitted
into the Society of Jesus, a little before their death.
He was executed at Tyburn, May 30, 1582.

Edmund Jennings

dmund Jennings was admitted into the English College at Rheims, under doctor, afterwards cardinal, Allen, and when he was twenty years of age, ordained priest. He was soon apprehended in the act of celebrating mass; and was executed, by hanging and quartering, in Gray's Inn Fields, the 10th of December, 1591.

In a very rare book of his life, printed at St. Omers, 1614, are several historical prints, representing the principal circumstances of his life and death. This work was published, at a considerable expence, by the Papists, in order to perpetuate the remembrance of two "Miracles," which are there said to have happened at his death. The first is, that after his heart was taken out, he said, "Sancte Gregori, *ora pro me.*" Which the hangman hearing, swore, "God's wounds! see his heart is in my hand, yet Gregory is in his mouth!" The other is, that an holy virgin being desirous of procuring some relick of him, contrived to approach the basket into which his quarters were thrown, and touched his right hand, which she esteemed most holy, from its having been employed in acts of consecration and elevating the host, and immediately his thumb came off, without force or discovery, and she carried it home, and preserved it with the greatest care.

Roger Filcock

oger Filcock (by Stow erroneously called Thomas) received his education at Seville, in Spain, where he was ordained priest, and soon after sent hither as a missionary. Dod informs us, that he and Mark Backworth, a gentleman who acted in the same character, were executed at Tyburn, the 27th of February, 1601, together with Mrs. Anne Line, who suffered death for harbouring and assisting missionaries.

Francis Page

Francis Page was born, according to some accounts, at Harrow on the Hill, in the county of Middlesex, or, as some others say, at Antwerp, which it seems he pleaded at his trial, which, however, was not regarded by his jury as the truth. Being in the profession of the law, he became clerk to a noted lawyer, where he fell in love with a young gentlewoman, through whose means he be came a Catholic, but in the course of his conversion, he not only renounced his profession, but likewise his mistress; as upon a motion of Father Gerard, he went over to Douay, and was ordained a priest, and sent to this country on the mission, where he had he knew. She had been converted to the Protestant faith, and now made it a practice to betray and cause to be taken up Catholic priests. The sight of this woman made him mend his pace, which she perceiving, made no less haste after him, calling out "Mr. Page, I want to speak with you." He would not seem to hear her, but stepped into the first open house, and shutting the door, desired the master of the house (who was a Protestant) to let him out by a back door, which he was about to do; when the woman coming up, knocked violently at the door, crying out "A Traitor! a Traitor! a Seminary Priest!" and raised a mob about the door; so that the man being afraid of the consequences, would not suffer Page to escape, but delivered him up. He was immediately taken to Newgate, brought to trial, found guilty, and was executed at Tyburn, April 20th, 1601.

Theobalds

The favorite residence of James I. originally belonged to the
Earl of Salisbury and Sanderson in his life of James mentions his stopping at Theobalds, in his first progress towards
London. How it came into his possession does not appear
whether as a gift or a purchase in Chaney's Hertford; notice
is taken of Theobald Steet, but none of the Palace.

James I.

James I

ames had not long been seated on the throne, before his religious principles became too well known to the Catholics, to leave them room to doubt his steady adherence to the reformed religion; the knowledge of which induced several desperate persons to frame a plot[1] that has never been paralleled in the

---

1   THE BEST HISTORICAL ACCOUNT IS GIVEN BY HUME, WHICH IS HERE TRANSCRIBED, IN ORDER TO THROW SOME LIGHT ON THE INTENTIONS OF THE PERSONS INTERESTED IN THE CONSPIRACY.

annals of any country.

We are now to relate an event, one of the most memorable that history has conveyed to posterity, and containing at once a singular proof both of the strength and weakness of the human mind; its widest departure from morals, and most steady attachment to religious prejudices. 'Tis the GUNPOWDER TREASON of which I speak; a fact as certain as it appears incredible.

The Roman Catholics had expected great favour and indulgence on the accession of James, both as he was descended from Mary, whose life they believed to have been sacrificed to their cause, and as he himself, in his early youth, "was imagined to have shewn some partiality towards them, which nothing they thought but interest and necessity had since restrained. It is pretended, that he had even entered into positive engagements to tolerate their religion, as soon as he should mount the throne of England; whether their credulity had interpreted in this sense, some obliging expressions of the king, or that he had employed such an artifice, in order to render them favourable to his title. Very soon they discovered their mistake; and were at once surprized and amazed to find James, on all occasions, express his intention of strictly executing the laws enacted against them, and of persevering in all the vigorous measures of Elizabeth. Catesby, a gentleman of good parts and of an ancient family, first thought of a most extraordinary method of revenge; and he opened his intentions to Piercy, a descendant of the illustrious house of Northumberland.

In one of their conversations with regard to the distressed condition of the Catholics, Piercy broke into a sally of passion, and mentioned assassinating the king; Catesby took the opportunity of revealing to him a nobler and more extensive plan of treason, which not only included a sure execution of vengeance, but afforded some hopes of restoring the Catholic religion in England.

In vain, said he, would you put an end to the king's life: he has children, who would succeed both to his crown and to his maxims of government. In vain would you extinguish the whole royal family: the nobility, the gentry, the parliament, are all infected with the same heresy, and could raise to the throne another prince, and another family, who, besides their hatred to our religion, would be animated with revenge for the tragical death of their predecessors. To serve any good purpose, we must destroy, at one blow, the king, the royal family, the lords, the commons; and bury all our enemies in one common ruin. Happily, they are all assembled on the first meeting of the Parliament; and afford us the opportunity of glorious and useful vengeance. Great preparations will not be requisite. A few of us combining, may run amine below the hall, in which they meet, and choosing the very moment when the king harangues both houses, consign over to destruction these determined foes to all piety and religion. Meanwhile, we ourselves standing aloof, safe and unsuspected, shall triumph in being the instruments of divine wrath, and shall behold with pleasure those sacrilegious walls, in which were passed the edicts for proscribing our church, and butchering her children, tossed into a thousand fragments; while their impious inhabitants, meditating, perhaps, still new persecutions against us, pass from flames above to flames below, there for ever to endure the torments due to their offences.

Piercy was charmed with this project of Catesby, and they agreed to communicate the matter to a few more, and among the rest to Thomas Winter, whom they sent over to Flanders, in quest of Fawkes, an officer in the Spanish service, with whose zeal and courage they were all thoroughly acquainted. When they inlisted any new conspirator, in order to bind him to secrecy, they always, together with an oath, employed the Communion, the most sacred rite of their religion. And it is remarkable, that no one of these pious devotees ever entertained the least compunction, with regard to the cruel massacre which they projected, of whatever was great and eminent in the nation. Some of them only were startled by the reflection, that of necessity many Catholics must be present, as spectators or attendants on the king, or as having seats the house of peers. But Tesmond, a Jesuit; and Garnet, superior of that order in England, removed their scruples, and shewed them how the interests of religion required, that the innocent should be sacrificed with the guilty.

All this passed in the spring and summer of the year 1604; when the conspirators also hired a house in Piercy's name, adjoining to that in which the parliament was to assemble. Towards the end of that year, they began their operations. That they might be less interrupted, and give less suspicion to the neighbourhood, they carried in store of provisions with them, and never desisted from their labour. Obstinate in their purpose, and confirmed by passion, by principle, and by mutual exhortation, they little feared death in comparison of a disappointment; and having provided arms, together with the instruments of their labour, they resolved there to perish in case of a discovery. Their perseverance advanced the work and they soon pierced the wall, though three yards in thickness; but on approaching the other side, they were somewhat startled at hearing a noise, which they knew not how to account for. Upon inquiry, they found, that it came from the vault below the house of Lords; that a magazine of coals had been kept there; and that as the coals were selling off, the vault would be let to the highest bidder.

The opportunity was immediately seized; the place hired by Piercy thirty-six barrels of powder lodged in it; the whole covered up with faggots and billets, the doors of the cellar boldly flung open, and every body admitted as if it contained nothing dangerous. Confident of success, they now began to look forward, and to plan the remaining part of their project.

The King, the Queen, Prince Henry, were all expected to be present at the opening of Parliament. The Duke, by reason of his tender age, would be absent, and it was resolved, that Piercy should seize or assasinate him. The Princess Elizabeth, a child, likewise was kept at Lord Harrington's house, in Warwickshire; and Sir Everard Digby, Rookwood, Grant, being let into the conspiracy, engaged to assemble their friends on pretence of a hunting match, and seizing that princess, immediately to proclaim her Queen.

So transported were they with rage against their adversaries, and so charmed with the prospect of revenge, that they forgot all care of their own safety; and trusting to the general confusion, which must result from so unexpected a blow, they foresaw not, that the fury of the people, now unrestrained by any authority, must have turned against them, and would probably have satiated itself by an universal massacre of the Catholics.

The day, so long wished-for, now approached, on which the parliament was appointed to assemble. The dreadful secret, though communicated to above twenty persons, had been religiously kept, during the space of near a year and a half. No remorse, no pity, no fear of punishment, no hope of reward had, as yet, induced any one conspirator, either to abandon the enterprise, or make a discovery of it. The holy fury had extinguished in their breast every other motive; and it was an indiscretion at last, proceeding chiefly from these bigoted prejudices and partialities, which saved the nation. Ten days before the meeting of parliament, Lord Monteagle, a Catholic, son to Lord Morley, received the following letter, which had been delivered to his servant by an unknown hand.

> My Lord,
> Out of the love I bear to some of your friends, I have a care of your preservation. Therefore I would advise you, as you tender your life, to devise some excuse to shift off your attendance at this parliament. For God and man have concurred to punish the wickedness of this time. And think not slightly of this advertisement; but retire yourself into your country, where you may expect the event in safety. For though there be no appearance of any stir, yet I say, they will receive a terrible blow this parliament; and yet they shall not see who hurts them. This counsel is not to be contemned, because it may do you good, and can do you no harm: for the danger is past, as soon as you have burned the letter. And I hope God will give you the grace to make good use of it; unto whose holy protection I commend you.

Monteagle knew not what to make of this letter; and though inclined to think it a foolish attempt to frighten and ridicule him, he judged it safest to carry it, to Lord Salisbury, Secretary of State.

Though Salisbury, too, was inclined to pay little attention to it, he thought proper to lay it before the King, who came to town a few days after.

To the King it appeared not so light a matter: and from the serious earnest style of the letter, he conjectured that it implied something dangerous and important. A terrible blow, and yet the authors concealed, a danger so sudden, and yet so great; these circumstances seemed all to denote some contrivance by gunpowder; and it was thought adviseable to inspect all the vaults below the houses of parliament. This care belonged to the Earl of Suffolk, Lord Chamberlain; who purposely delayed the search till the day before the meeting of parliament. He remarked those great piles of wood and faggots which lay in a vault under the upper house; and he cast his eye upon Fawkes, who stood in a dark corner, and passed himself for Piercy's servant. That daring and determined courage, which so much distinguished this conspirator, even among those heroes in villainy, was fully painted in his countenance, and was not passed unnoticed by the Chamberlain. Such a quantity also of fuel, for the use of one who lived so little in town as Piercy, appeared a little extraordinary; and, upon comparing all circumstances, it was resolved that a more thorough inspection should be made. About midnight Sir Thomas Knevett, a justice of peace, was sent with proper attend ants; and before the door of the vault finding Fawkes, who had just finished all his preparations, he immediately seized him; and turning over the faggots, discovered the powder. The matches, and every thing proper for setting fire to the train were taken in Fawkes's pocket; who finding his guilt now apparent, and finding no refuge but in boldness and despair, expressed the utmost regret that he had lost the opportunity of firing the powder at once, and of sweetening his own death by that of his enemies. Before the council, he displayed the same intrepid firmness, mixed even with scorn and disdain; refusing to discover his accomplices, and shewing no concern but for the failure of the enterprize.

This obstinacy lasted two or three days: but being confined to the Tower, left to reflect on his guilt and danger, and the rack being just shewn to him, his courage, fatigued with so long an effort, and unsupported by hope or society, at last failed him, and he made a full discovery of all the conspirators.

Catesby, Piercy, and the other criminals, who were in London, though they had heard of the alarm taken at a letter sent to Monteagle, though they had heard of the Chamberlain's search, yet they resolved to persist to the utmost, and never abandon their hopes of success: but at last, hearing that Fawkes was arrested, they hurried down to Warwickshire; where Sir Everard Digby, thinking himself assured that success had attended his confederates, was already in arms, in order to seize the princess Elizabeth.

She had escaped into Coventry; and they were obliged to put themselves on their defence against the country, who were raised from all quarters, and armed by the Sheriff.

The conspirators, with all their attendants, never exceeded the number of eighty persons; and being surrounded on every side could no longer entertain hopes either of prevailing or escaping. Having therefore confessed themselves, and received absolution, they boldly prepared for death, and resolved to sell their lives as dear as possible to the assailants. But even this miserable consolation was denied them: Some of their powder took fire, and disabled them for defence.

The people rushed in upon them; Piercy and Catesby were killed by one shot; Digby, Rookwood, Winter, and others, being taken prisoners, were tried, confessed their guilt, and died, as well as Garnet, by the hands of the executioner.

Notwithstanding this horrid crime, the bigoted Catholics were so devoted to Garnet, that they fancied miracles to be wrought by his blood; and in Spain he was regarded as a martyr.

Neither had the desperate fortune of the conspirators urged them to this enterprize, nor had the former profligacy of their lives prepared them for so great a crime. Before that audacious attempt, their conduct seems in general, to beliable to no reproach. Catesby's character had entitled him to such regard, that Rookwood and Digby were seduced by their implicit trust in his judgment; and they declared, that, from the motive alone of friendship to him, they were ready on any occasion to have sacrificed their lives. Digby himself was as highly esteemed and beloved as any man in England; and he had been particularly honoured with the good opinion of Queen Elizabeth. It was bigoted zeal alone, the most absurd of prejudices masqued with reason, the most criminal of passions, covered with the appearance of duty, which seduced them into measures that were fatal to themselves, and had so nearly proved fatal to their country.

The Lords Mordaunt and Stourton, two Catholics, were fined, the former ten thousand pounds, the latter four thousand, by the Star-Chamber, because their absence from Parliament had begotten a suspicion of their being acquainted with the conspiracy. The Earl of Northumberland was fined thirty thousand pounds, and detained several years prisoner in the Tower; because, not to mention other grounds of suspicion, he had admitted Piercy into the number of gentlemen pensioners, without his taking the requisite oaths.

The King, in his speech to the parliament, observed, that though religion had engaged the conspirators in so criminal an attempt, yet ought we not to involve all the Roman Catholics in the same guilt, or suppose them equally disposed to commit such enormous barbarities. Many holy men, he said, and our ancestors among the rest, had been seduced to concur with that church in her scholastic doctrines concerning the Pope's power of dethroning kings, or sanctifying assassination.

The wrath of heaven is denounced against crimes, but innocent error may obtain its favour; and nothing can be more hateful than the uncharitableness of the puritans, who condemn alike to eternal torments, even the most in offensive partizans of Popery. For his part, he added, that conspiracy, however atrocious, should never alter in the least his plan of government: while with one hand he punished guilt, with the other he would still support and protect innocence. After this speech he prorogued the parliament till the 22d. of January.* The moderation, and I may say magnanimity of the King, immediately after so narrow an escape from so detestable a conspiracy, was no wise agreeable to his subjects.

Their animosity against Popery, even before this provocation, had risen to a great pitch; and it had perhaps been more prudent in James, by a little dissimulation, to have conformed himself to it. His theological learning, confirmed by disputa-

46

tion, had happily fixed his judgment in the Protestant faith; yet was his heart a little biassed by the allurements of Rome, and he had been well pleased, if the making of some advances could have effected an union with that ancient mother-church.

He strove to abate the acrimony of his own subjects against the religion of their fathers; and, he became himself the object of their diffidence and aversion. Whatever measures he embraced, in Scotland to introduce prelacy, in England to enforce the authority of the established church, and support its rites and ceremonies, were interpreted as so many steps towards Popery; and were represented by the puritans assymptoms of idolatry and superstition.

Ignorant of the consequences, or unwilling to sacrifice to politics his inclination, which he called his conscience, he persevered in the same measures, and gave trust and preferment almost indifferently to his Catholic and Protestant subjects; and finding his person, as well as his title, less obnoxious to the church of Rome than those of Elizabeth, he gradually abated the rigour of those laws which had been enacted against that church, and which were so acceptable to his bigoted subjects: but the effects of these dispositions, on both sides, became not very sensible, till towards the conclusion of his reign.

At this time James seems to have possessed the affections even of his English subjects, and, in a tolerable degree, their esteem and regard.

Hitherto their complaints were chiefly levelled against his too great constancy in his early friendships; a quality which, had it been attended with more economy, the wise would have excused, and the candid would even perhaps have applauded.

His parts, which were not despicable, and his learning, which was great, being highly extolled by his courtiers and gownmen, and not yet tried in the management of any delicate affairs for which he was unfit, raised a high idea of him in the world; nor was it always through flattery or insincerity that he received the title of the second Solomon. A report, which was suddenly spread about this time of his being assassinated, visibly struck a great consternation into all orders of men; the Commons also abated of their excessive frugality, and granted him an aid, payable in four years, of three subsidies and six fifteenths, which Sir Francis Bacon said in the house, might amount to about four hundred thousand pounds; and for once the King and Parliament parted in friendship and good humour. The hatred which the Catholics so visibly bore him, gave him at this time an additional value in the eyes of his people. The only considerable point, in which the Commons incurred his displeasure, was by discovering their constant goodwill to the puritans; in whose favour they desired a conference with the Lords, which was rejected.

* The Parliament this Session passed an Act obliging everyone to take the oath of allegiance—avery moderate test, since it decided no controverted points between the two religions, and only engaged the persons who took it to abjure the Pope's power of dethroning Kings.

Henry Garnet

his prime engine, and in all probability the contriver of the Gunpowder-Plot, was artful enough to screen himself for some time, even from the suspicion of being concerned therein; until the confession of Bates, Catesby's man, implicated him in the general crime. He was, however, after his apprehension, according to some accounts, examined no less than twenty-three times, and it was in consequence of the following trick being put upon him that induced him to make an ample confession. Cecil, Earl of Salisbury, contrived to lodge him in a chamber adjoining that in which Oldcorne was confined, where they might converse through a chink in the wall, and be overheard by two men, whom he had placed in ambuscade for that purpose; the stratagem succeeded. Garnet was betrayed, confessed the treason, and was executed in St. Paul's church-yard, May 3, 1606.

Robert Catesby

obert Catesby, of Ashby, in the county of Leicester, was a gentleman of good property and estimation, and had so winning a manner, as to possess every one who knew him with a most extravagant liking to his company: insomuch, that several of the persons concerned in this conspiracy, frankly confessed they were drawn into it more in consequence of his persuasion, than any conviction in their own minds, of the propriety of the cause they had embarked in. Catesby entered with such spirit into this business, that in the course of a few months, he was obliged to call in some monied persons to carry it on with the spirit that was necessary. In consequence of which, with the advice and concurrence of Piercy, Winter, Fawkes, &c. he opened the plot to Sir Everard Digby, and after wards to Francis Tresham, Esq. the first of whom promised fifteen hundred pounds, and the latter two thousand, to purchase such materials as wanting to carry the plot into execution. Upon the discovery of Fawkes's apprehension, Catesby, in company of Piercy, the Winters, Wrights, &c. betook themselves to flight, and were overtaken at Holbeach, in Staffordshire, where, at the house of Stephen Littleton, after a desperate sally, Catesby and Piercy were killed with one shot. To this circumstance may be attributed the mystery that surrounds the Gunpowder Treason, as Catesby was the only person who could have given a satisfactory evidence, he being the only layman that Garnet, the superior of the Jesuits, would confer with on this subject.

Thomas Piercy

homas Piercy, the most particular and intimate friend of Catesby, was nearly allied to, and greatly in the confidence of the Earl of Northumberland, and was by him, as captain of the gentlemen-pensioners, admitted into that band without taking the customary oaths; for which omission, and the known intimacy that was between them the Earl suffered a tedious imprisonment of fifteen years.

Piercy was by far the most violent of the conspirators, and on one occasion, offered to rush into the presence-chamber and stab the king: but this was over-ruled by the more cautious Catesby, who then first opened to him his scheme of extirpating the whole royal family and nobles by gunpowder: to aid which purpose, Piercy engaged to furnish four thousand pounds out of the Earl of Northumberland's rents, and to provide ten swift horses in case of any emergency that might require speed. Upon the discovery of the plot, he betook himself to flight, and was killed with Catesby in the following manner: One John Street, of Worcester, who had charged his musquet with a brace of bullets, and resting it upon the wall by the gate, shot at them as they were coming in rank, and not in file, from the door to wards the gate each bullet, as he thought, killed a man; for which action the king gave him two shillings a day during his natural life, to be paid him out of the Exchequer.

Sir Everard Digby

ir Everard Digby was descended from an ancient family, resident at the time of his birth (1581) at Drystoke, in Rutlandshire. He was educated under the tuition of some popish priests, and his father dying when he was but eleven years of age, he was early introduced to the court of Queen Elizabeth, where he was much noticed, and received several marks of her Majesty's favour. On the coming in of King James, he went likewise to pay his duty, as others of his religion did; was very graciously received, and had the honour of knighthood conferred upon

Sir Everard Digby

him, being looked on as a man of fair fortune, pregnant abilities, and a courtlike behaviour. He married Mary, daughter and sole heiress of William Mulsho, Esq. of Gothurst, in Buckinghamshire, with whom he had a great fortune, which, with his own estate, was settled upon the children of that marriage. One would have imagined that, considering his mild temper and happy situation in the world, this gentleman might have spent his days in honour and peace, without running the smallest hazard of meeting that disgraceful death, which has introduced his name into all our histories: but it happened far otherwise. He was drawn in to be privy to the gunpowder-plot; and though he was not a principal actor in this dreadful affair, or indeed an actor at all, yet he offered 150l. towards defraying the expences of it; entertained Guy Fawkes, who was to have executed it, in his house; and was taken in open rebellion with other Papists after the plot was detected and had miscarried. The means by which Sir Everard was wrought upon to engage in this affair, himself affirmed to be these: first, he was told that King James had broke his promises to the Catholics; secondly, that several laws against Popery would be made in the next parliament, that husbands would be made obnoxious for their wives' offences, and that it would be made a præmunire only to be a Catholic; but the main point was, thirdly, that the restoring of the Catholic religion was the duty of every member, and that, in consideration of this, he was not to regard any favours received from the crown, the tranquillity of his country, or the hazards that might be run in respect to his life, his family, or his fortune.

Upon his commitment to the Tower he persisted steadily in maintaining his own innocence as to the powder-plot, and refused to discover any who were concerned in it; but when he was brought to his trial at Westminster, Jan. 27, 1606, and indicted for being acquainted with and concealing the powder treason, taking the double oath of secrecy and constancy, and acting openly with other traitors in rebellion, he pleaded guilty.

After this, he endeavoured to extenuate his offence, by explaining the motives before mentioned; and then requested that, as he had been alone in the crime, he might alone bear the punishment, without extending it to his family; and that his debts might be paid, and himself beheaded. When sentence of death was passed, he seemed to be very much affected; for making a low bow to those on the bench, he said, "If I could hear any of your Lordships say you forgave me, I should go the more cheerfully to the gallows."

To this all the Lords answered, "God forgive you, and we do." He was, with other conspirators, on the 30th of the same month, hanged, drawn, and quartered, at the west end of St. Paul's church, in London, where he asked forgiveness of God, the King, the Queen, the Prince, and all the Parliament; and protested, that if he had known this act at first to have been so foul a treason, he would not have concealed it to have gained a world, requiring the people to witness that he died penitent and sorrowful for it. Wood mentions a most extraordinary circumstance at his death, as a thing generally known, namely, that when the executioner plucked out his heart, and according to form held it up, saying, "Here is the heart of a Traitor," Sir Everard made answer "thou lyest."

He left at his death two young sons, afterwards Sir Kenelm and Sir John Digby, and expressed his affection towards them by a well-written and pathetic paper, which he desired might be communicated to them at a fit time, as the last advice of their father. While he was in the Tower, he wrote, in juice of lemon, or otherwise, upon slips of paper, as opportunity offered; and got these conveyed to his lady, by such as had permission to see him. These notes, or advertisements, were preserved in the family as precious relics; till, in 1675, they were found at the house of Charles Cornwallis, Esq. executor to Sir Kenelm Digby, by Sir Rice Rudd, bart. and William Wogan, of Gray's-Inn, Esq. In the first of these papers there is the following paragraph: "Now for my intention, let me tell you, that if I had thought there had been the least sin in the plot, I would not have been in it for all the world; and no other cause drew me to hazard my fortune and life, but zeal to God's religion."

Ambrose Rookwood

Ambrose Rookwood

mbrose Rookwood, like the majority of the conspirators, was a man of fortune, and, previous to this circumstance, of character unimpeached when called on to answer why judgment of death should not be pronounced against him, he answered, "though his offence was incapable of excuse, it was not altogether incapable of extenuation;" and the rather, in that he had not been either author or actor, in the business, but drawn in, to abet the same, from the extreme regard he bore to Catesby; whom he professed to esteem above any man he knew and concluded by observing, it was not the fear of death, but grief that so shameful a one would leave a perpetual blemish to after ages, on his name and blood.[1] Executed Jan.31, 1606.

---

[1] Bigotry to the Roman faith seems to have been inherent to this name (and perhaps family) as an Ambrose Rookwood was executed in the year 169— for being concerned in a plot to assassinate King William.

John Grant

ohn Grant, one of the conspirators, resident at Coventry, in company with several violent Catholics, broke open a stable, and carried off seven or eight horses belonging to Noblemen and Gentlemen of the place; with which assistance (thinking the explosion had taken place) he intended to obtain possession of the Princess Elizabeth, then on a visit at Lord Harrington's, but being frustrated in this scheme, he was taken, brought to trial and executed, with Sir Everard Digby, Robert Winter, and Thomas Bates.

John Grant

Francis Tresham, Esq

his Gentleman was one of the most considerable, in point of fortune, of the conspirators; and was early informed of the plot by Catesby and Piercy, as Sir Everard Digby and himself were the first monied men they called in to aid their purpose. Tresham, it appears, offered five hundred pounds more than Sir Everard, who proffered fifteen hundred, and Tresham, two thousand pounds, to purchase combustibles, hire the house, and pay for any assistance necessary.

After the apprehension of Fawkes, Tresham had the temerity to remain about the court, and the better to disguise his connection in the plot,

Francis Tresham, Esq

proffered his service for the suppression and apprehension of the other conspirators: but being suspected, he was examined, and sent to the Tower, where he confessed the whole, and within a few days after, died of the stranguary.

Robert Keies

obert Keies, as he expressed himself on his trial, was a man of desperate estate and fortune, and that his situation at the bar, was as good in point of circumstance as any he had known for a length of time. And but from the following anecdote, taken from Fuller's *Church History*, we might naturally suppose the temptation of money, rather than a wish for the advancement of religion, had prompted him to the undertaking.

A few days before the fatal blow should have been given, Keies, being at Tichmarsh, in

Northamptonshire, at his brother-in-law's house, Mr. Gilbert Pickering, a Protestant, he suddenly whipped out his sword, and in merriment made many offers therewith at the heads, necks, and sides of several gentlemen and ladies then in his company: it was then taken for a mere frolic, and so passed accordingly; but after wards, when the treason was discovered, such as remembered his gestures, thought he practised what he intended to do when the plot should take effect; that is, to hack and hew, kill and destroy, all eminent persons of a different religion from himself.

He was executed with Guy Fawkes and others, January 31, 1606.

Guido Fawkes

uido Fawkes, a Gentleman and an Officer in the Spanish service, was purposely brought from Flanders to assist in the mine, and fire the train under the Parliament-house. Upon the prorogation of the Parliament, he returned to Flanders, to consult with Owen and Sir William Stanley; the latter of whom had treacherously, and contrary to his oath, delivered up Deventer, a rich town in Overyssel, gained from the Spaniards by Robert Dudley, Earl of Leicester.

From Flanders, Fawkes went to Italy, and from thence came to England; where he passed for the

1. Bates
2 Robert Winter
3. Christopher Wright

4. John Wright
5. Thomas Percy
6. Guido Fawkes

7. Robert Catesby
8. Thomas Winter

servant of Piercy, under the fictitious name of Guy Johnson.

He was principally employed in placing the gun powder, faggots, &c. in proper order for explosion, and at the same time for concealment from too curious observation; as the doors of the cellar were left open for public inspection, to avoid suspicion.

Fawkes was apprehended at the entrance of the cellar-door, about midnight, by Sir Thomas Knevett, (a gentleman of his Majesty's privy-chamber, and a justice of peace in Westminster) who immediately carried him before the privy-council; be fore whom he affirmed, that had he been within the doors at the time of his apprehension, he would have blown himself up, with all those that were about him at the time.

He was afterwards examined at Whitehall; where no man, of whatever rank, was denied access or speech with him; and, notwithstanding the continued teazing, and impertinent questions that were put to him, it was observed, he neither changed countenance nor lost his temper the whole day; treating the better sort with contemptuous scorn, and jestingly mocking the rest.

He was from the council conveyed to the Tower; where although he was shewed and threatened with the rack, he still seemed fixed in his first purpose of denying any accomplice whatever; and it is asserted, he was prevailed on to make what confession he did from the following circumstance being told him, upon such authority as he could not doubt.

There was a Mr. Pickering, of Tichmarsh Grove, in Northamptonshire, who was in great esteem with King James. This Mr. Pickering had a horse of special note for swiftness, on which he used to hunt with the King. A little before the blow was to be given, Mr. Keies, one of the conspirators, and brother-in-law to Mr. Pickering, borrowed this horse of him, and conveyed him to London upon a bloody design, which was thus contrived. Fawkes, upon the day of the fatal blow, was appointed to retire himself into St. George's Fields, where this horse was to attend him, to further his escape (as they made him believe) as soon as the parliament should be blown up. It was likewise contrived that Mr. Pickering, who was noted for a Puritan, should that morning be murdered in his bed, and secretly conveyed away; and also that Fawkes, as soon as he came into St. George's Fields, should be there murdered, and so mangled, that he could not be known: upon which it was to be spread abroad, that the Puritans had blown up the Parliament house; and the better to make the world believe it, there was Mr. Pickering, with his choice horse, ready to escape; but that stirred up some, who seeing the heinousness of the fact, and him ready to escape, in detestation of so horrible a deed, fell upon him, and hewed him to pieces; and to make it more clear, there was his horse, known to be of special speed and swiftness, ready to carry him away; and upon this rumour, a massacre should have gone through the whole land upon the puritans.

When the contrivance of this plot was thus dis covered by some of the conspirators, and Fawkes, who was now a prisoner in the Tower, made acquainted with it, whereas before, he was made to believe by his companions, that he should be bountifully rewarded for that his good service to the Catholic cause, now perceiving, that on the contrary, his death had been contrived by them, he thereupon freely confessed all that he knew concerning that horrid conspiracy, which before, all the torments of the rack could not force him to do.

The truth of this was attested by Mr. William Perkins, who had it from Mr. Clement Cotton, to whom Mr. Pickering gave the above relation.

Guido Fawkes was executed with Thomas Winter, Ambrose Rookwood, and Robert Keies, within the Old Palace Yard, Westminster, not far from the Parliament-house, January 31, 1606.

Thomas Winter

his discontented Catholic had thoughts of quitting England for ever, and had retired himself to his brother's house in the country, till such time as a convenient opportunity should offer for that purpose. In the mean time he was twice sent for by Catesby, to come with all speed possible to London; where when he came on the second invitation, Catesby opened to him his gunpowder scheme, into which Winter readily entered, and almost as soon set off for Flanders, to sound the inclinations of several leading persons, towards such a scheme; where he was recommended to Fawkes, as a proper person to overlook the work; he being an approved soldier, and a skilful engineer.

They embarked at Dunkirk, and came to England together; soon after which Piercy hired the house adjoining the House of Lords, where they first began the mine.

Winter, in concert with the rest, retired to Staffordshire; where, at the explosion of powder that was laid in a platter to dry, he was scorched in so shocking a manner, as rendered him incapable of defence.

Some little time before this accident, Winter dreamt "that he saw steeples and churches stand awry, and within those churches strange and unknown faces."

And after, when the aforesaid explosion had, the day following, scorched divers of the confederates, and much disfigured the faces and countenances of Grant, Rookwood, and others, then did Winter call to mind his dream, and to his remembrance thought, that the faces of his associates, so scorched, resembled those which he had seen in his dream.

From the confession he made, he appears to have been very penitent, and resigned to his fate. Executed January 31, 1606

Robert Winter

obert Winter was drawn into this conspiracy by his brother Thomas; who, finding the persons first engaged in the mine insufficient to the task, proposed this brother as an assistant the rest might depend on; and at their condemnation he petitioned the court to suffer for both, as having been the means of his brother's misfortune.

Robert Winter escaped in company with Stephen Littleton, (owner of the house at Holbach, where the rest had taken shelter) and first found succour from one Perks, who secreted them in his barn; but doubting of their safety, they removed from thence, and were harboured by Humphrey Littleton, commonly called Yellow Humphrey, who was governor of the house in the absence of Mrs. Littleton, the owner thereof. Here they were not many days, before the cook of the house did much wonder what use Humphrey Littleton should make of so many dishes in his chamber at every meal, and, to satisfy his curiosity, went secretly to the door, and peeping through the key-hole, saw Stephen Littleton, and another man with him: at which sight he was so terrified that he knew not what to do; for to reveal them might endanger their lives, and to conceal them might cost him his own. After some debate with himself, he resolved to keep out of further trouble, and accordingly went and disclosed what he discovered to a relation; whereupon followed their apprehension and afterward their conviction, condemnation, and execution.

There was another brother of this family, John Winter, who was executed at Worcester, with Humphrey Littleton, Perks of Hagley, and Burford, his man; for receiving and entertaining Robert Winter and Stephen Littleton at the time of their flight, contrary to the King's proclamation.

John Winter employed a man at Warwick to learn on the trumpet the points of war, and kept him in pay for a month previous to the discovery of the plot.

John Wright

ohn Wright was one of the first persons to whom Catesby intrusted the secret of the plot; and they mutually agreed, that all who afterwards should enter on that business, should take the following oath; which was first administered by Catesby, Piercy, and this Wright, each to the other, at a house behind St. Clement's church, without Temple-bar:

"You shall swear by the Blessed Trinity, and by the Sacrament you now purpose to receive, never to disclose, directly nor indirectly, by word or circumstance, the matter that shall be proposed to you to keep secret, nor desist from the execution thereof until the rest shall give you leave."

He was killed, with a number of the other conspirators, in their desperate sally at Holbach, the place of their last resort.

Christopher Wright

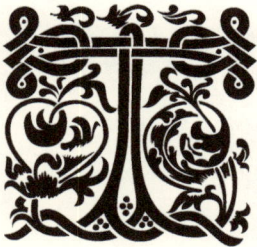

his person, like Robert Winter, was brought into the conspiracy by his own brother; and, from every circumstance that can be collected concerning him, was nothing behind the rest in forwarding this work of mischief.

It was Christopher Wright that first discovered the apprehension of Fawkes, and advised the conspirators to an immediate and separate flight; which advice, had they taken, it is more than probable that some might have escaped; instead of which, they imprudently resolved to raise the country into an open rebellion, and resort to that place which was to have been, their general rendezvous, had the explosion taken place: the consequence of which was, they were pursued, overtaken, some secured alive, and the rest killed. Among the last was this Wright and his brother.

Thomas Bates

oncerning Thomas Bates, who was Catesby's man, as he was wound into this treason by his master, so he was resolved, when he doubted of the lawfulness thereof, by the doctrine of the Jesuits. For the manner, it was after this sort Catesby, noting that his man observed him extraordinarily, as suspecting something of that which he the said Catesby went about, called him to him at his lodging in Puddle-Wharf, and in the presence of Thomas Winter, asked him what he thought the business was in which they were concerned, for that of late he had so suspiciously and strangely marked them. Bates answered, that he thought they went about some dangerous matter, whatsoever the particulars were. Whereupon they asked him again, what he thought the business might be; and he answered, that he thought they intended some dangerous matter about the Parliament-house, because he had been sent to get a lodging near unto that place. Then did they make the said Bates take an oath to be secret in the action which being taken by him, they then told him that it was true that they were to execute a great matter; namely, to lay powder under the parliament-house, to blow it up. Then they also told him that he was to receive the sacrament, for the more assurance; and thereupon he went to confession to Tesmond, the Jesuit; and in his confession told him, that he was to conceal a very dangerous piece of work that his master Catesby and Thomas Winter had imparted to him, and said he much feared the matter to be utterly unlawful; and therein desired the counsel of the Jesuit, and revealed to him the whole intent and purpose of blowing up the parliament-house, upon the first day of the assembly, at which the King, the Queen, the Prince, the lords spiritual and temporal, the judges, the knights, citizens, and burgesses, should all have been there convened and met together. But the Jesuit, being a confederate therein before, resolved and encouraged him in the action; and said that he should be secret in that which his master had imparted unto him, for that it was a good cause: adding, moreover, that it was not dangerous unto him, nor any offence to conceal it. And thereupon the Jesuit gave him absolution; and Bates received the sacrament of him, in the company of his master Robert Catesby, and Thomas Winter.

When condemned, he craved pardon, as being ignorant of the consequence of what he had concealed, and as being led into it by his Master, Tesmond, and Winter; he was however executed January 22, 1606.

Appendix

Appendix

otwithstanding the detection of the Gun-powder Plot, and the severity of the laws against Seminary and Missionary Priests, the Jesuits about the year 1614, encouraged by the Spanish Ambassador, Count Gondamor, held frequent meetings at the house of one Lovet, a goldsmith, in Fetter-Lane, who had a printing-press in his house for popish books; which were artfully distributed, through the means of the following persons, who in a pamphlet published about this time, intituled *Vox Populi*, are called Jesuits and Jesuited Priests. In this book is a very scarce and curious print, with the following inscription: "The Portraiture of the Jesuits and Priests, as they use to sit at council in England, to further the Catholic cause. Dr. Bishop, Dr. Bristow, Dr. Wright, F. Palmer, F. Wood, F. Lurtice, F. Maxfield, F. Higham, F. Sweete, F. Ployden (or Plowden), D. Smith, F. Lovet, F. Anineur, F. Worthington, F. Porter, F. Pateson."

The following accounts of these Persons are chiefly extracted from Dod's *Church History*.

Dr Bishop

illiam Bishop, who was born at Breyles, in Warwickshire, studied at Oxford, and in several foreign universities. He was employed in England as a missionary, in the reigns of Elizabeth and James I. in both which he suffered imprisonment for acting in that capacity. He was consecrated bishop of Chalcedon, at Paris, the 4th of June 1623, and invested with ordinary power to govern the Catholic church in England. He was esteemed a man of abilities, and was a very active and useful instrument to his party. He wrote several pieces of controversy against

Mr. Perkins and Dr. Robert Abbot, and published Pit's book *De illustribus Angliae Scriptoribus*. His gentle and amiable manners gained him esteem with men of all persuasions. He died the 16th of April, 1624. He was the first of the church of Rome that, after the Reformation, was sent into England in an episcopal character.

Dr Bristow

ichard Bristow, who was born at Worcester, was educated in the university of Oxford, where he and Campion entertained Queen Elizabeth with a public disputation, and acquitted themselves with applause. He shortly after conformed to the church of Rome, and was invited by the famous Allen, afterwards cardinal, to Douay, where he distinguished himself in the English college, as he did afterwards in that of Rheims, in both which he held considerable employments. The following character of him was found by Dod among the records in the former of these colleges; "He might rival Allen in prudence, Stapleton in acuteness, Campion in eloquence, Wright in theology, and Martin in languages." His death was occasioned by severe application to his studies.

𝔒r 𝔚right

r. Wright, in the list of the names of Romish priests and Jesuits, resident about the city of London, 1624, is said to be a grave ancient man, treasurer to the priests, and very rich. He was probably a different person from Dr. Thomas Wright, who was reader of divinity, in the English college at Douay, and author of the book "Depassionibus Animae," and several noted pieces of controversy. The latter, who, according to Dod, does not appear to have been a missionary here since the reign of Elizabeth, died about the year 1623.

𝔉ather 𝔐axfield

od mentions a person, whose name was Thomas Maxfield that studied at Douay, where he was ordained priest, and sent upon a mission into England, in 1615, and executed the eleventh of July, the following, on account of his sacerdotal character.

Father Higham

ohn Higham, who, for the most part lived abroad, employed himself chiefly in translating religious books from the Spanish.

The last of his works mentioned by Dod, is the *Exposition of the Mass*, which is dated 1622.

Father Sweete

ohn Sweete, a native of Devonshire, studied at Rome, where he entered into the society of Jesus, in 1608.

He was sent on a mission from Rome to England, in the reign of James, and died at St. Omers, the 26th of February, 1632. He is said to have been the author of *A Manifestation of the Apostacy of M. Ant. de Dominis*, printed at St. Omers, 1617, in 4to. Dr. Daniel Featly, who was his opponent in a disputation, has introduced him in his *Romish Fisher caught, or a Conference between Sweete and Fisher*. Lond. 1624.

Dr Smith

Dr. Richard Smith, bishop of Chalcedon, appears, according to Dod's account of him, not to have borne any ecclesiastical character in England before the year 1625. It is therefore very probable, that another Dr. Smith is here meant, and especially as the two following persons of the name are mentioned in the list of Romish Priests and Jesuits resident about the city of London, in 1624. "Dr. Smith, senior, some time of the college of Rome, and author of divers pestilent books; and Dr. Smith, junior, author of divers other books no less dangerous."

A strong party was raised against the bishop of Chalcedon, by the regular clergy, who loudly accused him of infringing their privileges. This forced him to abscond.

Father Worthington

Thomas Worthington, who was born at Blainscoe, near Wigan, in Lancashire, studied at Oxford and Douay, where he was president of the English College.

He was afterwards several years at Rome, and was some time apostolic notary. Being desirous of seeing England again, where he hadformerly been an active Missionary, he obtained leave to return thither, and shortly after died, in 1626.

He wrote annotations for the Douay Bible, in the translation of which he had a principal share, and was author of several books mentioned by Dod. *His Catalogus Martyrum in Anglia*, &c. was sold at the high price of eleven shillings and six pence, at the sale of Mr. Richard Smith's library, in 1682. The original price of this pamphlet was no more than sixpence.

Of the Jesuits, Palmer, Lurtice, Ployden, Lovet, Anineur, Porter, and Pateson, no other notice is taken, but of their being artful, and designing priests.

The laws against Seminary Priests, towards the end of James's reign, were in a great measure laid aside, for which the following anecdote is given as the cause. The King was extravagantly fond of hunting, in which exercise he would often outstrip his attendants for several miles: in consequence of this carelessness of his person, he was admonished in a letter "entirely to leave off the chace of Animals, or cease the hunting of Jesuits and Priests." James adopted the first pursuit, which he continued to enjoy the remainder of his reign.

FINIS

Index